MW01243094

WHO'S THE MAN?

HOW TO ACHIEVE GREATER SUCCESS THROUGH
SELF MASTERY

I dedicate not just this book but my life to my son Austin James Platt. Austin You are the absolute best thing that has ever happened to me in my life. From the moment I learned that you would be gracing this world with your presence, my whole existence has been to give you all you deserve and more. You have made me so happy and proud to be your father and I just hope that I have made you just as proud to call me your dad.

Love you, buddy

Contents

SECTION ONE THE MAN 4

INTRODUCTION 5

CHAPTER 1 THE MAN 6

CHAPTER 2 DISCOVER YOUR TRUE SELF 9

CHAPTER 3 VALUES 15

CHAPTER 4 REPEATING MISTAKES 23

CHAPTER 5 MEDITATION 28

CHAPTER 6 DISCOMFORT AND YOU 33

CHAPTER 7 HABITS 39

CHAPTER 8 HOW TO FIND YOUR PASSION 45

CHAPTER 9 TRAUMA 51

CHAPTER 10 ACTIVATION 57

CONCLUSION 62

SECTION ONE
THE MAN

INTRODUCTION

With everyone living life on the surface, the questions abound as to who exactly a man is and how he can harness all of what is inside him to achieve greatness and fulfill his life purpose. Every man who seeks to be great must have asked himself this question at some point. Discovering the answer to this question gets a large percentage of life's problems solved as it serves as a compass to help one surf through life successfully.

In this book, I seek to answer life's most difficult questions beginning with who you are and how this book can help you discover yourself. Knowing your values, strength, and weaknesses, how to avoid repeating the same mistakes, knowing how your mind works, handling discomfort, habits, and traumas, finding your passion, and eventually giving you the techniques to learn more about yourself.

This book isn't like the average self-help book you buy and sit on your coffee table, hoping to impress women when they come over. This is a life manual—if you may. A book that will send you on a life-transforming journey that will help you live as a fulfilled, spiritual, and fully integrated man.

CHAPTER 1
THE MAN

Who is the man?

Life has a lot of questions, and most times, these questions can seem like there are no answers. One of the many questions we are posed in life is, "WHO'S THE MAN." As cocky as it may seem, you see this question; it is more along the lines of "who are you?" I ask myself this question all the time, who's the man? Who is the man in the mirror? Who's the man in this physical form? Some say we are eternal beings living in multiple dimensions at once. Some say we are God himself, existing on earth as mortals. While some say we are just flesh and bones, and when we die, that's it, lights out. Only you can answer that question for yourself, who are you? The reason I cannot answer this profound question is that I'm not in your body, and neither am I experiencing what you are experiencing. Your life and experiences are yours. If I were to answer that question for you, I would only be able to take an educated guess, but it will still do you no good.

To find out who you are, you need to live your life. When I say live your life, I do not mean waking up and preparing for your day kind of life. It goes way beyond this.

We have two experiences at the same time; an inner one and an outer one. I have observed that we have let our external experiences define our lives or how we live our lives. We base what we do now on what we have done in the past, and in doing this, we are bound to keep experiencing the same things, to keep taking the same actions, and exhibiting the same behaviors. This will only lead us to re-living the same vicious cycle. This is a very limiting way to live, as we will miss out on so many beautiful things that await us. It is in the inner world where all things are possible, where all things exist, and where all of life is created and finished. Everything happens in one place, that infinite source where we all come from. It will serve you best to look within and live from "this place." It will be in error and to your detriment if you let the outer world influence you to believe this is all there is, and this is all you can be, do and have. I write this book not just for you but, more importantly, for myself. At some point, we must wake up to the truth of the matter; this is the reality of the world we live in. It may be hard for you to grasp because you have probably spent most of your life just like I have at a certain level, and you can't seem to get past it. It feels like you are stuck. You can't seem to level up and get over the hump. That is the purpose of this book, **to help you and me.**

I do believe that it will take us a few sets of new mind tools to enable us to develop new habits that will send us over the top because I don't know about you, but I am tired of peeking over the fence of million-dollar homes and seeing people eat at the big tables. I am tired of walking past fancy restaurants, looking in through the window, and watching people eat lobster and steak. Well, I don't do all these I mentioned, LOL, but speaking metaphorically. And please do not get me wrong, I have been in some high places and tasted the fruit of success, but I haven't been able to stay there long enough to savor the moment fully. And I have been at some low points, too, the lowest of lows. I am proud of these low times because, during those times, I saw what type of man I was. I saw what I was really made of. Just my humble beginnings would have dictated that I wouldn't have made it this far. I would have been in jail or even dead by now. So I am grateful to be here with you.

Before I go ahead, I want to share a little bit of my story. I am the youngest of two, and I have an older sister. I was born and raised in Flint, Michigan. I loved my city, and all that made my childhood worthwhile. I was raised by my mom and stepfather well enough through sacrifice and hard work. Even though I lived in the hood, I attended a private school, and it was a blessing as it gave me a sense of purpose and a sense that there was something bigger than me and the little bubble I was raised in. I will share with you some of my most valuable life experiences in hopes of connecting with you on a much deeper level.

CHAPTER 2
DISCOVER YOUR TRUE SELF

The struggle to discover one's self has never been more real than it is now. With all the noise surrounding us, from social media to the unnecessary pressure put on us by those we love and society at large to make something out of our lives. It is a chore nowadays to quieten down and discover who we are.

The journey of getting to know yourself may be more than a little boring, I mean, what else is there to learn? You have spent every second of your life with yourself, and there definitely can't be any surprises, right? Well, If you feel this way, then you are not alone. You know a lot less about yourself than anyone else in your life knows.

We do not know ourselves well, and most of us don't want to know. We fear what we might discover about ourselves. We avoid examining ourselves, and we would rather watch tv, eat snacks, surf the internet or binge-watch our favorite series. Like a vampire to a mirror, we do everything to avoid knowing the truth about ourselves. And that's the way they want it. They want us so distracted that we lose ourselves completely.

As unpleasant as the truth may be, only you hold the secret to greater levels of success.

When you understand and discover who you are, you can;

- Gain control over yourself
- Avoid your mistakes and common pitfalls

- Understand and deal with your negative habits
- Have healthier relationships
- Choose a life path that suits you
- Find love and happiness

Most of us are suffering from some mistaken identity. We've bought into the American dream like it's one size fits all. We've bought into everything that society has designed for us, like some stereotypical, predestined path chosen for us to follow. We work jobs we do not like, but we just can't figure out what else to do! We repeat the same mistakes and still have no clue as to what we are doing wrong. At times, we find out that we are headed for doomsday but cannot explain why we do what we do and how to correct all our mistakes.

"Success is much more challenging without self-knowledge."

To be highly successful, you need to;

- Set big goals that are meaningful to you
- Utilize your strength and avoid your weakness
- Deal with stress in a productive manner
- Know how to motivate yourself
- Overcome fear
- Persevere

These will be easier to accomplish when you know yourself. Without self-knowledge, luck becomes more of a factor.

Your true self is that part of you that is constant. It is that part of you, It is that part of you that makes you unique, which differentiates you from the rest of the world. It is the unadulterated you, the "you" that you would be if you were free from the unnecessary pressures and cares of life. The "you" that

10

you would be if you had no attachments to the opinion of others. It is the 100% real deal. It is the "you" without worry, doubt, and fear.

Self-knowledge is essential. It allows you to work through from a deep place- from the deep, dark corners of your subconscious mind.

~Mec Roseff

Discover your true self lurking beneath the surface of your fear and erroneous beliefs

One thing that has hindered many people from discovering who they are is fear. Most of us often have allowed fear to cripple the best chances we've had to make an everlasting impact on our society, starting from our immediate environs. This fear is also seen in our knowing so little about ourselves. Fear has a crippling effect on our lives as it stops us from reaching our full potential. To reach our potential effectively, we need to know who we are. In knowing who we are, we can connect with fear and have its voice silenced.

Another thing that has stopped a lot of folks from reaching their full potential is the beliefs they have been made to take up as the truth. These beliefs are not just erroneous but have also kept people bound in a particular box that shouldn't define them. It has led them to believe that they can only come so far, even if they can outdo their status. This belief is very limiting and has made men define themselves based on what others have to say and what is expected of them from society. This belief comes from other sources we have been exposed to, stemming from societal pressure that expects us to behave in certain ways. Interestingly enough, this too is a leading cause of depression in high numbers.

In this chapter, I seek to restructure your thinking and realign you to live way above this fear and limiting beliefs. To do this, you should answer the questions that follow subsequently.

1. What would my dream profession be if I knew I'd succeed and no one would judge me negatively. In answering this question, we search deep into our hearts to know what we yearn to do and admits the noise of what is trending. For example, you may want to be a rap star, and so many factors seem to point you to the reasons why you can't. Some beliefs could be that you believed for too long that you are less capable than you are. Also, at this point in your life, you're too old and it might be too late to become a rap star. But having this strong desire that you really want to become the next Jay Z could point you to who you truly are.

2. Whom do I admire most? Most times, we emulate the people we love a lot. Take your time to look around you and look at your life too. You will discover that you copy those you admire a lot.

3. This shows that the people we admire say a lot about our personalities. Look closely around you. Who are those people you admire and stalk, LOL? Look at them, how they think, how they act, even how they dress. You will share the same ideologies with them. This says a lot about your personality.

4. What are my greatest accomplishments? Man is in love with the idea of being accomplished. We naturally love that a project or idea has our names written bodily on it, screaming this is our work. You've might have done things you are not proud of. Never mind that instead look at some of the successful projects you've worked on. Look at the things you have accomplished. It doesn't have to be something so big that keeps the world in perpetual awe. It could be charity work, community service, etc. But whatever it is, look closely at it. It somehow speaks a lot about who you are.

5. Remember, your name came to be emboldened on a particular work, and somehow, you are not proud of the job. So the

focus should be on things you've done in the past that you were excited about. This can help you define who you are.

6. What am I ashamed of? We all have that moment where we did things totally embarrassing. We remember those moments and wish they never happened. Understand that what you might be ashamed of being associated with, another might belong to be part of it.

7. What have you done that you regret? What things from your past would you rather keep a secret? What can you learn from these experiences you are ashamed of?

8. So in defining these embarrassing moments and moments that brought us much shame, we can discover who we are and share the rest of our thoughts on the findings we get from this little exercise.

9. Describe the ideal Man? We all have this picture of the perfect man. In answering this question, try to factor in some basic things, which include how this man will dress, how he looks, his career, the industry he should be in, what his life values will be, etc. In writing down the ideal man, we can comfortably point out and figure out who we truly are and what areas of life we need to enhance.

Maybe you share the same values as this ideal person. This says a lot about who you are.

In answering these questions, do understand that it is personal. The aim is to find out who you are; hence there is no correct or wrong answer. This is not some high school exam where you are graded by some scheme, but rather this is an exercise that will help you become the best you can be. So you must be sincere with yourself to get the best out of it.

Your true self also has the ability to experience the full spectrum of emotions. You see, in life, I found out its fundamentals, and the pure intention behind living is happiness. This doesn't dilute that we are encumbered by so many emotions, and they can all come at once and leave us in a state where we cannot understand what is going on. Not everyone might want to be happy, but for me, I just want to find happiness in all that I do. This does not downplay the role of other emotions in defining who we are because sandwiched between happiness are other emotions; the feeling of sadness, depression, and anger. In experiencing all these emotions, we get to fully understand and discover who we are. This is because, in these times, we may not predict what exactly we would do, but in experiencing these, we reveal to ourselves who we are. This is where your true self lies, in the bliss of all these emotions.

CHAPTER 3
VALUES

Man, no matter where you are, lives by some set of values. These values define us as we make critical decisions about our lives based on what we value.

According to the Advanced English offline dictionary, values are the beliefs of a person or a social group in which they have an emotional investment either for or against something.

Our value defines us. Values tend to mimic rules that govern our lives and shape our thought patterns.

Everyone has values they live by, only that some values can make you while some other values can mar you. So invariably, I can see your values in the decisions you make every day, starting from what you eat, to what you wear, to the books you read, to the people you hang out with. All of man's activities on earth are governed by values.

Here are values that can make you a better person

• Honesty This may sound cliché, but an honest person stands the chances of succeeding more than a man that is dishonest. This is relatively true as honesty begins by being true to yourself, An honest person is not disposed to cheat or defraud. They are not deceptive. These values breed trust amongst those you will work with as they are certain that you are not in a hurry to rob them of their goods or money. This value will also be seen in your decisions as you are very mindful of it. So in being honest, you are first honest to yourself before you are honest to and with others.

- Integrity A man of integrity is a spiritual man. Integrity is a state of undivided, unbroken completeness. It is also a state of moral soundness. This is a very vital value as it shapes the life of anyone who embraces it. It screams professionalism in anything one embarks to do. This is because life has a way of teaching us the craziest stuff. Our way and our integrity can leave us unscathed, helping us finish strong and bold no matter what it is that we face.

- Punctuality This is high on my values list, and a lot of folks seem not to care anymore. It doesn't matter if your appointment is online or offline. You should never be late. Be on time!! And whenever you are late, pre-inform those who should be aware. It keeps your reputation.

- Hard work/Smart work Laziness has never paid off. To make the transition you need to make in life, you need to put in some degree of work. It doesn't matter the position. The work you put in will determine if you will make that transition to the top or not.

- Responsibility This is a trait of trustworthiness. It is being accountable or answerable to someone for something or being responsible for one's action. This is the ability to believe in a cause and work towards achieving that cause. It's like a force that binds you to something and gives you the ability to make that thing work without giving excuses, no matter the challenges you may face. This value will keep you on your toes and gain you a lot of respect as people are sure that whatever you set out to do, you will do it well.

- Respect Everyone wants to be respected but to get respect, you need to give respect. It's like a system that churns out what you give it. So it is respected in, respect out. Give respect to everyone you meet, but this doesn't mean you should let people treat you like trash. Set the boundaries and give them the ultimate respect they deserve. In doing this, you get your own respect in return.

• Compassion This is where Empathy and sympathy come in. In a world full of evil and misunderstanding, be the one that understands others. Whereas sympathy is understanding someone's situation because you have been there before, or you can imagine what it is like to be in that situation, empathy is showing compassion to someone even when your mind can't wrap itself around the situation at hand. This will make you be that go-to man when people are challenged, as they see you as the one who will understand and lend a helping hand.

Your values can change. Yes, you can change your values. It doesn't matter if you haven't built this set of values over the years. You can imbibe them all and watch your life transform into something beautiful. And probably you're scared that people will talk, they will talk, but then you have a life to live, a purpose to fulfill. It then means that whatever they have to say as you make this transition and imbibe all these values to become a better man doesn't matter if their words are more critical and judgmental than encouraging.

Remember that your values will reflect on the decisions you will make and how you will live your life generally. It means you need to imbibe values that will get you to your desired destination.

Strength and weaknesses

Every man, even those we deemed the strongest, is laced with both strengths and weaknesses. And this makes our individual lives beautiful. The strengths and weaknesses form a collateral beauty for those who know how to leverage and harness their strengths and understand their weaknesses.

Now let's think together. Can you remember your best friend in high school, remember how he ruined his relationship by some

17

mistakes, or think about your mom and the things she couldn't do.

You see how easy it was for you to remember them, now think and reflect on your own life. What can you say your weaknesses are? What do you think you need to change to achieve success?

Now ask a few of your friends who are true to you and intentional about seeing you succeed. You will find out that their answers are almost the same. Their answers may not be pleasant, but deep down, you know they are telling the truth.

I get it. I understand It is more exciting and easier to discover your strengths than to put in the work to understand your weaknesses. As Men, we've attached this ill and evil sentiment to weaknesses, and most times, we do not want to hear that we are weak or lacking in any area of life. So we instinctively and consciously avoid our weaknesses.

But here, in this chapter, I seek to show you how you can leverage your strengths and understand your weakness.

Ask yourself these questions.

What am I naturally good at? Like with every other question you will answer here, you must be true to yourself. It behooves you then to take responsibility and be true to yourself. This is where your transformation will begin.

So what are you good at? See, I'm in love with music but suck at playing instruments or singing. It doesn't downplay my love for music; I am not naturally good at it. I may learn it along the way, but it isn't my natural talent or ability.

The same thing goes for you. You may be in love with something, but it isn't your natural strength. We all individually have that thing that comes to us naturally. It could be music, sports, science, business, etc. It comes to you so naturally and easily that you can do it without batting an eyelid.

We all have at least one or two things that come to us easily. List these natural strengths.

What have I learned to be good at? From the time we are born, we unconsciously learn and pick up one or two traits we see around us. From speaking to walking to eating, we all learned something. For example, maybe you have always loved science, you have always been intrigued by animals, man, plants, and the atmosphere, what have you invested time and resources to learn?

Make a list of all these things you have learned; these will form your strengths. Remember, these are not innate skills, talents, and abilities, but skills you have developed.

What do my friends and family view as my strength? In asking friends and family this question, you might be surprised at the answers you will get. The reason their opinions are valid as to what your strengths are is simply a result of their association with you. They have stayed with you long enough, engaged in conversations with you, and can tell comfortably your interests and strengths.

What have others complimented me for? Have you ever been where you are working on something with someone for the first time, and he commends you for something you did? This could be your strong area.

Try to remember the compliments you have received over time and write them down.

These are your strengths and can be harnessed to your advantage.

What are my hobbies? What are the things you love to do? Our hobbies are a demonstration of what brings us to the state of happiness, and the goal is always to connect to happiness.

For some people, they would rather spend time swimming, and this is how they relax. Whereas others love extreme sports. For some, sports isn't their thing at all. They would rather spend time reading or tucked away in a laboratory.

What people spend their time on differs, and that thing tends to be their strong area.

What activities can cause me to lose track of time? Have you ever engaged in an activity that should end at a particular time only to look up, and time has flown by?

Now you have a comprehensive list of your strengths. It is important to identify your strengths and interests as it is easier to be successful. This will help you use your strengths to your advantage and make a mark.

Just like it is important to identify your strengths, it is also important to know your weaknesses. Weakness either needs to be remembered or avoided. It's like embarking on a journey, and you remember that a section of the road was washed away last month by a flood. You are most likely going to take another route to avoid it or try to find out if it has been fixed. The same thing goes for our weaknesses. In identifying your weaknesses, you give yourself the option of either avoiding them or trying to fix them.

Here are questions that will help you understand your weaknesses

What is that thing or those things that every other person seems to do better than you? There are things you are naturally gifted with and other things quite challenging for you than others. Maybe no matter how hard you try, you make no headway in that thing.

List these things. That could be your weakness.

What do I find challenging to learn or improve at? There are some things that, no matter how hard we try to learn; we never seem to learn.

This isn't particular to you; everybody has that thing they have tried learning but couldn't quite get the hang of it. Not because they didn't put in the effort, but because it isn't their thing. Add this to your list of weaknesses.

20

What do my family and friends view as my weakness? As with our strengths, our friends and family also have a say. The reason is they have been with us long enough to know our strengths and weaknesses.

So take this question to your friends and family and hear what they have to say. Most times, you will find out that their answers are the same. This shows you your weaknesses.

Push them to be honest with you. As it might be easier for them to tell you your strengths than to point out your weaknesses. They are doing this so they won't look judgmental, but to know the truth about your weaknesses, you will need their honest answers.

What hobbies do you detest? You might have heard that all hobbies are good as they help relieve stress, but deep down, you know there are some hobbies you can never attempt to try. You naturally dislike these hobbies.

It could be playing cards, bowling, hunting, etc. The things you dislike could reveal your weaknesses. If you can't get yourself to do them, it could be your weakness.

Also, look for similarities amongst the things you dislike. What is the common thread?

What activities make you miserable and drain your energy? Have you ever decided to try out something for the first time, and rather than it being an exciting journey and experience, it left you miserable and drained all your energy? It could range from attending parties or social events to sports, cultural activities, meeting new people, etc.

These activities could be your weakness or reveal your weakness.

What five careers sound like pure torture to you? It could be accounting, finance, medicine, geology, etc. As much as you've been made to believe that all careers are equal, the thought of these careers makes you cringe.

Also, ask yourself what these careers have in common and the skills needed in these careers. Is it that you lack these skills or that it doesn't give room for adventures? In answering these questions, you not only discover your weaknesses but also give yourself valid reasons you have these weaknesses.

Learn your weakness and understand them. Doing this is very critical to your success. Not knowing them is like walking into a bear trap when trying to achieve a big goal. Learning your weaknesses will help you go around these traps or fortify yourself to go through the traps.

Remember that someone else is strong in these areas you struggle in and that success is not a solo journey. You can learn to leverage your strengths to attain success.

"Who looks outside, dreams; who looks inside, awakes."

Carl Jung

CHAPTER 4
REPEATING MISTAKES

We all make mistakes; mistakes will always be part of our journey to success. But it is not the occasional mistakes we make that derail us from attaining success, but the habitual mistakes we make. These mistakes seem to have become part of us, and sometimes we are unaware of them. We can spot these mistakes from a mile away in others but never notice them in ourselves. The thing about these mistakes is that we make them repeatedly. We often view these areas where we make these mistakes as bad luck. But luck, whether good or bad, is evenly distributed across humanity. If you have an area where you seem unlucky consistently, then you are making one or more mistakes repeatedly.

To discover these mistakes, you will need help from family members and friends.

Analyzing these areas of your life can help you avoid making the same mistakes over and over

•   Review your life from beginning to end Take a count of all the times you became miserable and depressed at times when your life was chaotic. Look where you failed and flopped at something. Be critical in doing this. Check the events that occurred before the failure. You will discover something common about those times.

-       What did you do or fail to do?

-       What were you thinking?

-       Where did you go wrong?

-       Did you see any pattern of incorrect thought or action?

-       What would have been a better course of action?

Answering these questions will bring to your remembrance certain occurrences and things you did when you failed. You will discover what the common denominator was during those times and hopefully avoid them in the near future.

•   Relationships Look at your failed relationships, both romantic and unromantic relationships. Include your relationship with your family members too.

Think back on every major disagreement you had. What was the contributing cause to that disagreement, especially the quota you contributed?

Consider all your relationships that have ended. What did you do that somehow led to the end of that relationship?

Examine your romantic relationships critically. What was the commonality amongst the partners you've had? Are you choosing the wrong type of people for yourself?

While answering these questions, be sincere to yourself. Your sincerity will lead you to the path of truth, and this path is where your success lies.

•   Finances Are you struggling financially, or have you ever struggled with your finances? Look at those times when you were low on cash and resources or when you almost faced bankruptcy. What led you to that situation? What did you do or fail to do that had you in that mess? What financial and buying decisions did you make that led you to be broke? Is there something you could have done differently to salvage or avoid that situation?

•   Health Our health is crucial to our attaining success in life. You will discover that a healthy man is more likely to become successful than one on a hospital bed. The state of your health adds up to make you a whole man. What mistakes have you been making as it has to do with your health? Are you eating healthy, or do you eat based on what you crave? Do you visit your doctor regularly for a medical checkup? Are you prone to certain diseases yet still do everything that can make you fall sick? Have you cut down on your carb and junk intake and embraced veggies? Do you exercise regularly? All these sum up to help you live a healthy life. Do you make fatal health mistakes? What mistakes are you making daily that keep your health and fitness less than acceptable?

• Work What mistakes are you making at work that could cost you your job? Do you come late regularly? Do you do your job below the excellence bar? Do you dress like a bum to work? Ask co-workers and your boss about the mistakes they have noticed that you make. Their answers may reveal things you never knew.

The mistakes we make every day are our greatest anchors to failures. They sabotage us continuously, and most times, we are unaware of them. Discovering and fixing these mistakes is a huge step towards success.

Mistakes on their own are inevitable, but it is by constantly making the same mistakes we remain in the same position. While some people notice and learn from their mistakes, others have no idea that they are making mistakes, let alone learn from them to better their life.

These four areas are the major areas of life that happen to us every day. They form the bedrock of our existence, and in seeking the mistakes we've made in time past, we can take hold of the future and achieve whatever success we want to achieve. Starting from the people, we want to have in our lives; friendships and romantic relationships inclusive, to how we will relate with these people to make the future blissful. Down to being in control of our finances, what to buy and what not to buy, where to invest in and where not to invest in, where to live and where not to live, business to start, and businesses that might drain our pockets without achieving its desired goal, making profits. It will also help us identify ways to lead a healthier lifestyle. This is possible as we know the food to avoid and the ones to eat. It also will help us visit our doctors regularly, exercise as often as we should, and generally live healthier. It will also help us maximize our work environment and keep us in the good books of our boss. Avoiding these work mistakes will make us more productive at work, and we will perform more excellently than we used to.

Answering these questions as honestly as possible will help us make better choices as it has to do with our lives and ultimately, we can avoid all these mistakes that have left us hopeless and feeling unlucky.

Big mistakes can also turn out too big events that eventually shape our lives.

Like I said earlier, we all make mistakes. This life's journey we are all embarking on is littered with challenges, and in handling these challenges, we may drop the ball from time to time. It takes a strong man to handle the unpredictable nature of getting things wrong. At times it feels like you are in that zone where nothing can go wrong, and boom Fumblerooski, you find yourself making the very mistake you wanted to avoid, and you wonder how it all happened. Next thing your mind tries to work a solution out of the whole mess. It is those who learn quickly from mistakes and bounce back that can leverage the knowledge gathered from that experience that can turn the big mess into a great event. The truth is that some mistakes leave us more demoralized than some other mistakes. But these more demoralizing mistakes can be the big turn we are seeking. It could be from these lowest moments we will make drastic decisions that will change the course of our lives forever.

As a man, learn to see the good in every situation. You may have hit rock bottom from that mistake, but it is time to stop bemoaning yourself and bounce right back. The truth is that you stand at a better advantage than the person who has never tried. You now have an experience they will never have. You know what exactly not to do to fall back into that trap or get yourself into that mess again. And even if you make another mistake try again, and remain resilient and firm in your decision to succeed.

The problem is not with failing or falling. The problem is remaining in that failed state.. There is greatness waiting for you, and in your failure, you build the character needed for the journey ahead. Private failures all sum up the big picture. Always keep that big picture in front of you and watch how all of these failures come together to form a collateral beauty that men will admire.

Look around you at all the successful men you have heard about. It may look like life never gave them a deadly punch that should have sent them packing to the pit beneath, their success in the fact that they stayed through. Mistakes are part of the process. Embrace them like a Valentine teddy bear and see the brighter picture.

You've always got to be aware of why you don't win;
otherwise, you'll keep losing

Layne Beachley

CHAPTER 5
MEDITATION

Meditation is not an activity left just for monks alone. Everyone can and should meditate. In meditating, we gather the ability to manifest and become more powerful. There are things I have been able to manifest quite unbelievable. I believe that once you meditate, your mind clears and focuses better. The mind being full of so much information is like land littered with sticks and debris. In meditation, you gather the sticks together and trash the debris and dirt. This leaves your mind and thoughts much more organized. I didn't realize until later in life how powerful meditation is. Contracted focus holds a power so strong that the universe will assist in bringing your desires towards you. Had I found out about the power of meditation long before now, I would have been in a different place in my life. But here I am, and here you are. You can begin to taste the fruits of being a better person by using this amazing tool.

When I started meditation, three minutes was excruciating. But with constant practice and sitting down to save my life, I can meditate for up to twenty minutes twice a day (Transcendental Meditation), and it will seem like a few seconds just went by. If there is one habit I can recommend, it is meditation.

Meditation comes with many benefits that can affect different aspects of your life.

Some of its emotional benefits include;

- Gaining a new perspective on stressful situations
- Building skills to manage your stress

- Increasing self-awareness

- Focusing on the present

- Reducing negative emotions

- Increasing imagination and creativity

- Increasing patience and tolerance

These are some of the emotional benefits of meditation. There are more, but in meditating, we harness our image abilities and connect with the spiritual.

Meditation was initially meant to deepen the understanding of the mystical and sacred forces of life. But now, we've discovered it can also be used to relax and relieve stress. It can also be employed by sick patients whose conditions are worsened by stress. Some of these conditions based on some researchers include; asthma, anxiety, cancer, chronic pain, depression, insomnia, tension headaches, etc.

In meditation, you focus your attention on important thoughts and get rid of thoughts that may be causing you so much stress. Here you clear away loads of information stored up daily in your mind. Meditation is a type of contemporary mind-body medicine.

For me, I believe this world began as a thought. It began in the mind (Universal Consciousness); hence the mind is the birthplace of dreams and creativity. Out of the mind comes infinite possibilities. Through meditation, you can control, create and build the life of your dreams. The world is full of distractions. More like the reality we live in is a garbage dump. Daily, you are sifting through the minds of others as well as yours. Hence taking that time out every day to get away from the noise and sort out your thoughts is much more beneficial.

Our minds differ greatly from what they appear to be. There is a way things seem to be, and there is a way it actually is. We all have a different worldview, the thoughts and noise going on in our minds taint our perspective, and we cannot see the world beyond the filters changing our perspective. Meditation is, therefore, one way to notice the activity and bias of the mind. It is also a way to give your mind a well-deserved rest.

There are various types of meditation, and they include

- Guided meditation In this meditation, you mentally picture things, situations, or places you consider calm and peaceful.

- Mantra meditation Here, you keep repeating a word, a phrase, or a sentence to keep away distracting thoughts.

- Mindfulness meditation It involves having an increased awareness about living in the present. Here you can focus your mind on what is happening as you meditate, such as the rhythm of your breathing.

- Qi gong This combines meditation, relaxation, and breathing exercises to restore and maintain balance. It is part of traditional Chinese medicine.

- Tai Chi This is a form of gentle Chinese martial arts. Here you practice a set of self-paced series of postures or movements slowly.

- Transcendental meditation This allows your body to fall into a state of profound rest and relaxation and your mind to achieve inner peace. In this meditation, you repeat a particular mantra, such as a word or phrase in a specific pattern.

- Yoga Here, you perform postures and controlled breathing to achieve a flexible body and a calm mind.

Elements of meditation

Different types of meditation require different elements to help achieve their maximum effect. Some of which include

- Focused attention
- Relaxed breathing
- A quiet setting
- A comfortable position
- An open attitude

Everyday ways to practice meditation

I will advise that you meditate for at least 5-10 minutes every day. Here are ways that can make the journey easy for you.

- Breathe deeply
- Scan your body
- Repeat a mantra
- Walk and meditate
- Engage in prayer
- Read and reflect
- Focus on love and gratitude

Building your meditation skills

As with every other skill, meditation is learned. It does not happen overnight. So even if your meditation skills are poor, do not judge them. It will only add to the stress you are trying to avoid. Practice makes expertise. So keep practicing. Remember also that no matter how long you have been meditating, your mind could wander off too. All you need to do is to bring your mind to what you were focusing on and continue with your meditation. Experiment with different kinds of meditation till you find the one that suits you. Adapt your meditation to suit your need at that moment. Always remember there is no right or wrong way to meditate. Just engage in meditation.

CHAPTER 6
DISCOMFORT AND YOU

I was listening to a famous actor named Matthew McConaughey being interviewed, and he said that sometimes we must lean into our discomfort.

We have all been in situations quite uncomfortable and been in challenges that took us away from our comfort zone. Discomfort is simply a feeling of not being comfortable. We can never do away with discomfort, but how we handle discomfort reveals the content of our hearts. It shows us the stuff we are made of.

It is crazy to think we can avoid discomfort as if the beginning of our lives weren't uncomfortable. It was uncomfortable for your mom to birth you, and for you, it was strange to leave the comfort of the womb to be ushered into a world you were never aware of. The whole of the world and life isn't meant to be a comfortable experience.

Life is about growth, and the process of growth is uncomfortable. Growing is like being stretched; you may not break, but you will feel the pain of being pulled. In growth, your mental capacity is stretched to accommodate more experiences and knowledge. And to get the best out of life, you need to grow.

There is the right way to handle discomfort, and there's the wrong way to handle it. Here are ways you are probably handling discomfort that does not benefit you

1.   What are you most likely to do when faced with a task you do not feel like doing? Let's say you are to do the dishes, and somewhere deep down inside of you, you hate doing

the dishes. What is the most likely thing you'd do? Will you find another activity to do that is more agreeable to you? Will you take a nap? Or will you do it? Will you rationalize that it can wait till tomorrow? Do you psych yourself up so you can get it done?

2.   Boredom and how you handle boredom? Those moments you have nothing to do, what do you do? Watch TV? Do you choose a goal and work on it? Eat something delicious or text a friend?

3.   What is your response to stress? We all have been stressed in our lives. How did you or do you respond to stress? Do you drink, eat or sleep? Or do you relax and then work on a goal that will lead you to your desired success?

4.   What are your bad habits? All negative habits provide one solution; they make you feel better in the short term. There are no other benefits to bad habits. Bad habits also are a way of dealing with negative emotions. So most times, when you develop a bad habit, you do it because you were trying to run away from an uncomfortable situation.

How do you deal with discomfort? The answer to this question says a lot about you. Poor and inadequate responses to discomfort make life more challenging and decrease the chances of success. Handling discomfort appropriately gives you a huge advantage over those who do not.

Here are better ways to handle discomfort.

1.   Find a solution When faced with a very uncomfortable situation, seek a solution to the problem rather than try to avoid it. This will make you much more powerful.

2.   Relax This doesn't mean taking a nap or ignoring the situation on the ground. This is about finding ways to

reduce the discomfort you are feeling while seeking the solution you can act on.

3. Exercise This may sound crazy, but exercising works. It can help reduce the stress you are feeling while engaging your mind with possible solutions to the problem at hand. It also keeps you fit; hence it isn't causing any harm, nor is it wasting your precious time.

4. Have a glass of really cold water In the heat of the moment, a glass of cold water can calm you down and relax your nerves. Asides from this, water is healthy, so you have nothing to lose drinking water.

5. Have a staring contest with the challenge This doesn't sound like what you want to do, but when faced with a challenge that seems to threaten your peace and comfort, all you may need to do at that moment is to take a seat and stare right into the face of the challenge. Instead of doing something harmful or worthless, sit with the discomfort and observe it. How does it feel? Does it have a location in your body? Just maybe, the discomfort will fade away.

Discomfort is the body's way of trying to protect you, and it isn't okay if your life is at risk. But most times, it just pushes us to a place of panic and anxiety. Your ability to handle discomfort will tell if you will succeed or not.

Become aware of how you handle discomfort and devise better ways to cope. Like a fish out of water, you must grow lungs to breathe on land, and as a man released into the ocean, you must be ready to find ways to breathe underwater.

In handling discomfort, your mind is super important. You cannot avoid uncomfortable situations, but you can always navigate your way through every single uncomfortable situation and get yourself to that point where discomfort and the uncomfortable situation can be turned in your favor. Start by having a positive mindset. This always helps. Keep your mind occupied with things and situations that are positive only. This doesn't mean you should be living an illusion and in some fantasies that will never come true. You should preoccupy your mind with activities that will keep your energy high and positive.

Do you remember when I told you about how you should tap into your inner self in order to find out who's the man? I mentioned that I was in a lot of highs and lows in my life, and one low is this story I am about to share with you right now. In life, there are stories or experiences you can say to yourself, "I am not proud of that moment in my life," while there are some that will always be in your heart as an experience you know you didn't hate because it was an experience that created the period that defined you, and that is what the year 2014 was for me. I found myself homeless. And when I say it was a very trying time for me, it really was. Life was so bad for me, so much that I had no choice but to live in my car for a year.

Do you know the "weird" thing about it all—if I may call it weird. A lot of my close friends didn't even know about my situation. I decided to push this bolder back up the hill on my own, not because I was embarrassed or ashamed about where I was but because something inside was telling me this was a good thing and this would ultimately shape my life. I knew I could handle it and I'm sure you know that not everyone who hears about all the challenges you are going through will help you. Also, I didn't want to inconvenience anyone with my problems. I believed I would get through it with time, and if I rushed the process, I wouldn't learn what I needed to learn in order to become the man I wanted to be. That year brought so much hardship, along with my divorce, my stepfather was very sick and I was financially unstable. Having to get my own place and separate from my wife and son was the hardest thing I have ever had to do because divorcing was contrary to my nature. The next thing I knew, I was down, all the way down! and it lasted longer than I expected. Next I got evicted from my apartment, but luckily for me, I had a car. My car became my home. I would go to my then job at 24-Hour Fitness in Burbank, California and after working full day in sales, I would workout, take showers and go to my car a sleep. On my off days I would travel across town to spend time with my son and then return to the parking lot and spend the night. I repeated this process for a year. Through it all I always found a way to enjoy myself while I endured the process of claiming the title of being king of my life. Crazy as it may seem I felt alive, I felt an intense drive to keep going on. In the words of Lauren Hill "every day is another chance to get it right". My son, my young king, was the major driving force behind me not giving up. I never lost hope that things would get better for me. I knew deep down I was a good man, a good person, and I have always had the idea that because I am inherently good, eventually, things would work out for me.

Handling discomfort is a mental thing. You have to have a strong mind. Your mind must be your best friend and motivator. If it's not your best motivator, don't let your mind be the opposite— your main antagonist! You have to develop a strong optimistic mindset in all you do. You have to see the glass as full always. If it isn't, you should always find a way to refill every single day. I am a strong advocate of gratitude, the acceptance of where you are in your life is a key outlook to have. Learn to appreciate the little things, and you will see how far you have traveled and how much you have accomplished throughout your journey. I surrendered to my discomfort to the point where it became comfortable. During that period of time, my boss at the 24-Hour Fitness gym heard that I was living in my car and working there at the same time. He called me to the office and told me he had seen me going to my car to sleep and asked if I needed some help. I respectfully turned down his offer. "No, sir, thank you so much for your concern. But I know I am here for a reason, and it is necessary for me to be here. And if I rushed the process, I wouldn't learn what I was in this position to learn. See I believed that life always teaches us different lessons, and when it is was time for me to progress to the next stage in life I would be moved from my situation into a better one. I walked out of his office and went back to my car.

Now, what did I learn from this hardship? I learned never to judge a book by its cover. During that time I had to resort to begging for money outside of a 99cent store. Because of my homelessness, I view the homeless differently. Don't judge them because it could be you, because it was me. I learned that in life, nothing is guaranteed. I don't care if you have a million dollars or 5 dollars to your name, we are all one move away from sleeping in a car, I also learned that Downfalls don't happen suddenly; they happen gradually. Usually, they are the culmination of little mistakes made over an extended period of time. Now I can look back a see all the little mistakes I made that led to my downfall.

Because of those periods of hardship I am stronger mentally than Ive ever been. I strongly believed as long as I'm alive, I still have a very great chance of getting right back up. Material things will come and go. People will come and go. You must learn to have your own back, and be your own motivation, be your own support system first, and then the right people and circumstances will come along to assist you.

If you are in a low place in life right now, and you are reading this. I want to tell you to embrace it because **there is a lesson in the discomfort.** Don't try to rush out of it. Stay set, meditate and lean in. Find comfort in the discomfort, and you will come out of it stronger, wiser, and more resilient than ever before.

CHAPTER 7
HABITS

Let me ask you this, "Have you ever taken up a new interest, set a personal goal and crushed it? Have you made going to the gym a mandatory part of your day? if you answered yes to these questions, I say congratulations because you have created a new habit for yourself! That aside, as you start this new process of learning, you will see how beneficial, wonderful, and refreshing it is to set a new goal and achieve it. So in learning any new thing as liberating as the above, you will notice you are changing yourself for the better. If that isn't inspiring and empowering to you, then I don't know what to tell ya. What does all this mean? It means good habits are created—or formed—behind many positive changes. So in this chapter, the good habit I will be focusing on is repetition. Building and incorporating repeated actions and forming them into good habits will help you grow exponentially in your personally and professional life.

Habits are like a force of nature. Creating a new habit or working with a new habit helps you grow in ways you cannot imagine. Habits can be found deeply rooted in our subconscious minds. The subconscious mind is the mind that puts the body into action. Our mind is a very creative tool for making things work for us and otherwise. The mind propels us in motion towards or away from our goals. Your habits will become your rituals. First thing in the morning, what do you do? If you cant answer this question, that means you don't know your habits. There are certain early morning rituals you do, sometimes without even thinking too much about it. So, look out for these "little things" for example do you wake up and go straight to brush your teeth, or do you check your phone as the first thing you do when you wake up from sleep? How do you put on your clothes for the day? Do you put your pants on first or wear your shirt first? Do you go straight to the bathroom or straight to the kitchen? If you can be conscious of your morning habits and do something each morning to break the patterns you begin with, I assure you, you can rewire your brain to attract different experiences for the day. Some people say that early morning is the best time for new habits to manifest. Let me tell you my thoughts on this ideology ? First, the earth is fresh, barely touched by your feet in the morning, and the morning is the best place for everything new to start. The atmosphere is clear of the conglomerate of thoughts floating in the misty air, and that is exactly where new things begin. Life is at its purest form early in the morning. So, if you can make a habit of getting up by 5 a.m. at least every morning, this will form much of your new morning ritual that will become your habit, improving your life tremendously.

How to turn your rituals into habituals

I want you to please try and remember these three words; repetition, repetition, repetition. Repetition is the hammer that hits the nail in the coffin.

All these mentioned above are the root of learning the secret to cultivating good habits. Now, the ideal way to go would be to ask what the next step is in becoming something better. The simple and straightforward answer is **REPETITION**. The idea here is that if you keep doing something repeatedly, you will automatically get better at that thing. The key is to make it a habitual way of doing that thing. That's the challenge. Discipline, focus, and desire—are 3 keywords you should remember when forming a new habit (good habit). Your desire to learn them and have them shape the way you think is very remarkable. Desire is the first thing to have in mind when you want to change a thing and create a new habit. When you have the desire, that means you have the ability to create something different in your life. The next

40

is the focus. By focusing on the things very important to you, you will be on track with the change you want to make for yourself. The next thing you should remember is discipline. If you have the desire to make a change in your life, and you do all you can to stay focused on the change, to remain on track with "your change," you will need to stay disciplined through it all. What does this mean? To make sure you have your new habit learned, you will need the complete discipline of your mind and body. Your unique purpose is what will get the car—the habit—started. Igniting your car, is the desire to change, and your hands on the steering wheel, eyes fixed on the road and never looking back, is having the right mindset—FOCUS!

Becoming the man I am, has always been attributed to forming good habits. from a very young age, as young as when I was in grade school, my mother has always made sure she instilled in me good habits so that I would become a man who is respected and loved by others. All these great things can only come when a man's foundation is built on good values and habits. Seeing how many ills were happening to children around me when I was growing up, my mother knew that instilling the right values and teachings was a necessity . My mom unknowinling had this belief that your tongue is mighty and the words you speak can change your life. She strongly believed that her children were destined for great things, and they should always speak good to themselves. So, every day before school, she would tell us to say words of affirmation. "I AM A LEADER AND NOT A FOLLOWER was one of her favorite phrases." She would make us say this before we stepped out of the door each day. She made us repeat it often and wouldn't let us go until she felt it in her heart that we also believed what we were speaking to ourselves. It was an amazing feeling for me! I felt great speaking to myself, too my innermost self. I loved the way It made me smile whenever I stepped out of the house for school, and it was not just for school alone. She made us say, what I now know as Affirmation every time we were

41

about to leave the house, and still to this day I speak to myself in this way . It is now a very important part of my life. It is my secret sacred habit,

So, for my mom, it wasn't just going to end with saying words of affirmation, For her it was making sure we got to see the big picture, and that was exactly what I saw, it was amazing!

The key to increasing the odds of being successful is creating goals aligned to your purpose and values, then creating habits that bring you closer to your goals.

Consider how your habits can make or break your chances for success

1. What is your morning routine We all have a morning routine we work with, whether it was planned or not. By default, our mind has been programmed to act in a particular way. Whether we did that consciously or not is up to us. Your morning routine begins from the time you wake up. Look at your life; you will notice that you wake up every day at a particular time. It also includes what you have for breakfast. If you do not have a meal menu you follow, you are most likely going to have the same thing every morning. Your morning routine also encompasses what you do and think about in the shower. Do you brush your teeth before you shower, or do you do the opposite? Do you engage in thoughts of how the day will go or do you allow your mind to wander? Do you listen to music or do you listen to audiobooks? Do you review your plan for the day? Do you review your goals? Do you prepare on time to arrive at work on time? These sum up what your life will look like in the near future.

2. What do you do in the first two hours at work? What you do during the first two hours at work may be insignificant when looked at, but when engaging in that activity

consistently will show if you will be a productive staff or not. It will reveal over time if you will always deliver your work in time or not. Do you spend the first few hours at work having meaningless conversations with other staff? Or do you surf through the net for irrelevant things?

3. What is your routine when you get back home from work? Most people have a change of clothes and hit the couch to watch TV or hit the dining table. What you do with this time is crucial to being successful. What could you be doing each night differently to make the biggest difference in your life?

4. What do you do with the last two hours of your evening? Do you learn something new each night? Do you review your goal and to-do list for the day? Do you take action towards achieving the big picture? Do you prepare for the next day by setting new goals and getting your to-do list ready? Are you spending this time wisely?

5. What do you do during the weekends? Most Americans live for the weekend. So basically, the life cycle of an average American is to hustle during the week, then the club and party all weekend. No plan or investment into their future. Our weekends are our most flexible time, but for some, rather than spend this time wisely and make investments towards their future, waste it on nothing worthwhile.

Understand your habits and how they impact your success. Poor habits lead to poor results, while good habits produce billionaires and other super successful people. Think about your current situation and predict what your future will look like based on these habits.

After evaluating your current habits and predicting what your future will be like, it will be to your advantage if you discover that this isn't the future you want to have and that you can change your current set of habits to fit into that perfect future picture. Changing your habits need not be an uphill task, but daily make conscious efforts to see that you are taking steps, no matter how small, to the greater end.

This will, therefore, begin by having a clear picture of the future you would want to have. Until this clarity is attained, you may never have the courage to make the transition.

The next thing will be to work on your morning and night routine. You can add affirmations and meditation to your morning routine while you read books and take courses in the evening just before you go to bed. Also, if you have a 9-5 job, your evening time can be spent investing in knowledge and taking actions toward financial independence and security.

The next step will therefore be to make the most out of your weekends. You have more time on your hands during the weekends than on weekdays. It means you can invest that time wisely to add paint to the big picture.

The transition to forming new habits doesn't have to be so difficult. Take it one step at a time and watch yourself become that person that can fit into that big picture.

Also, learn to consistently repeat these actions you intend to make a habit. It is in the consistently repeating them that the habit is formed. Do something repeatedly and you'll become better at it. Remember, practice makes experts.

So it starts with having a desire, and that desire is birthed by having a big picture. Your big picture should be the purpose you are living for. After this desire comes goals and, finally actions. These actions are the habits you will build, and they are built by discipline. That is consistently repeating certain things that will help you become the person fit for the big picture.

CHAPTER 8
HOW TO FIND YOUR
PASSION

Let's look at my story in the previous chapter; you will notice that one of my driving factors is passion. I was passionate about something, about my future, and what I intended to achieve. This inspired me to meditate, speak positive words over my life, and spend time learning what I needed to learn about my beautiful future.

As a child, you probably had dreams and aspirations. Things you wanted to do when you grew up. You were very enthusiastic about it, and you basked in the euphoria of the thought. This dream was always on your lips wherever you went; then, life happened to you. You were hit with the sad reality that things aren't always the way they seem. You discovered that to achieve this desired goal, you need to put in a lot of work. Maybe you also found out that the trajectory and times were changing rapidly, and to fit into the changes sweeping through, you had to either discard your old dreams or modify them to suit where the world was headed. It may also be that you lost faith in that dream and lived your life pleasing people.

But I tell ya, it's not too late to rekindle that passion or discover a new one. Somehow we handled this topic when we talked about strengths and weaknesses, but right now, we will be specific and direct as to how you can find your passion. One thing you will need in the journey to discovering your passion is intentionality, and the other thing is sincerity.

To find your passion, ponder these questions and answer them truthfully.

•   If you were the last person on earth, what would you want to do or learn? This question eliminates the opinion of others as you will be answering this question based on what you want to do. Also, in answering what you would love to learn, you are answering it primarily on the benefits it will bring to you. So once again, you are not answering it based on what it will do for others but rather what it will do for you.

•   What is that one big thing you would love to achieve before you die? Death is an inevitable occurrence. According to biology, all living things die. So with this in mind, what is that one thing you intend to achieve on earth before the natural course of death happens to you? For some, it could be climbing Mount Everest, and for another, it could be finding the cure to cancer or any other deadly disease. For the guy who wants to climb Mount Everest, it shows a person enthusiastic about adventure, travel, risk, and physical challenges that exert so much on the body. Whereas for the guy who wants to find the cure to some disease, he is probably more interested in helping the society, intellectual challenges that exert much on the mind, and probably prefers to work in solitude than in a social setting.

•   What does your dream accomplishment say about you? Goals and dreams that provide a similar reward will be a major turn-on for you as they somehow make you feel a certain way. For example, someone who enjoys hiking will enjoy mountain climbing or biking. This is because they all involve physical exertion and leaves you feeling the same way.

What are you passionate about? Keep this question before you all the time, and you will be amazed at the answers you will produce. Keep a record of all the answers you get and do well to go back to them regularly.

Journaling

Journaling is a great habit to imbibe in the journey of discovering who you are. Every day of life, we see various thoughts about who we are, who we want to be, what we have achieved, what we want to achieve, what we've learned, and what we want to learn. In paying attention to what we think about every day, you will find a consistent pattern and calling towards a particular thing. It is therefore expedient we journal daily. This is because our thoughts can be effervescent, always bubbling, and could sometimes evaporate. Putting this off to another day may mean we will lose certain thoughts to this very nature of our thoughts.

Journaling is a great activity and;

- It is inexpensive. All you need is a pen and paper

- It is revealing. You will see the patterns in your thinking, life, and behavior.

- It is convenient. It can be done anywhere. Just when you get the idea, bring out your pen and paper or your gadget and write it.

- It is therapeutic. If you have ever tried writing things down, you will discover that you will have inner peace and joy. It is more like you get to release all the stress and anxiety you are experiencing on the paper. And be sure that the paper is always ready to take all you give it. It can be a listening ear when you have none.

- It gives clarity. When you journal things, you gain clarity on what you should do.

- It helps to monitor your progress, especially when embarking on a project.

- Use these strategies to start a journaling habit and learn more about yourself

1. Write with paper and a pen rather than a word processor Except if you are physically unable to write, it is best to write with paper and a pen. It gives you an experience you won't get using a word processor or document.

2. Review your day Remember journaling should be done daily. One way to ensure that you are journaling daily is to review your day. What new thing happened to you? Did anything out of the ordinary happen? What thoughts do you have about the day? Was it good or bad? Is there a way it could have been better? Did you reach your goal for the day?

3. Rate how you feel, both mentally and physically, on a scale of 1-10. Do you feel tired or drained? How often has this happened? How many times did it happen in a row? Have you taken any action towards it? Write it down and monitor it.

4. List your successes and failures Life is littered with so many successes and failures. Most times, we may forget what we have achieved so far in life and lose track of when life dealt us a deadly blow. Therefore, it is important to keep a proper record of your successes and failures. Document your journey through life. Journaling your successes and failures is one step towards attaining more successes and keeping your failures to the barest minimum. As it can help you to recognize your mistakes and discover ways to avoid them.

5. Review your progress Especially when working on something, journal your progress. Keep an accurate record of what you have done so far and what you intend

to do. Reviewing your goals keeps them fresh in your mind.

6.   Write down any other thing that seems relevant. It could be a concise story of how your day went. Or how someone got you annoyed. It could be about the things you wished you had, or certain positions you want to attain in life. Just do yourself the good of always writing down things as they come to your mind.

7.   Once every two weeks, go through all you have written in the past two weeks. As you do this, write down your thoughts about all you have written over the past two weeks. The things you wished you did better, incidents you wished never happened. Generally, review everything that happened. With this new information and insights you have, you can now see what you can do with the information. Will you change your schedule? Will you be more punctual to work? Will you read more books? Will you get better sleep? Will you avoid unnecessary dramas? The purpose of journaling is not just to have a journal but to help you gain direction and clarity on what next to do.

Keeping a journal can be intimidating as we naturally may not be interested in looking at ourselves closely. This should let you in on the importance of having a journal.

There are certain signs you may see that can point you to the need for a journal and excuses people give for not keeping a journal. Some of these includes

•   A journal is too dumb

•   I am too tired to write anything today

•   Keeping a journal is worthless and time-consuming

Any excuse you may give for not wanting to keep a journal is a valid reason to keep a journal.

Writing Prompts

Consider adding writing prompts to your self-discovery tools. Writing prompts are ideas and questions that can help direct your thinking and writing. Below are a few writing prompts to start you;

— If I had an extra hour every day, how would I spend it?

— What was my favorite job of all time? What did I like most about it?

— What do I want my obituary to say about me?

— With unlimited time and money, what career will I pursue if that is the only way I can spend my time?

— What more do I need in my life?

— What do I not want in my life?

— How do I believe others will describe me?

There are other writing prompts available, and you may add them or create your own. Adding a writing prompt daily to your journaling process will help you discover more about yourself than you already know.

This section is geared toward helping you discover who you truly are, and journaling and writing are crucial to achieving this purpose. Beginning with chapter two, you will discover there are tons of questions that will guide you towards discovering who you are. And to effectively answer these questions, you will have to write them down. So in the journey of self-discovery, journaling is the ink without which the pen cannot write.

CHAPTER 9
TRAUMA

Traumatic experiences can be very exhausting and can lead one to become suicidal, depressed, and a whole lot of other mental health issues. Trauma, especially childhood traumas, can negatively affect our thoughts and behaviors. It is like dirt underneath the rug of our consciousness. No one sees the experiences, but they see the behavior their experience has caused.

Trauma could mean different things to different people; hence almost everyone has been through some trauma, especially during childhood. For some people, their most traumatic time was having to deal with a bully in school, and this experience can make them feel insecure, less of themselves, or feel inadequate. For others, it could be the loss of a pet or a loved one, say a sibling or a parent. Due to the emotional connection they had with this person, they may find it difficult to love or let themselves feel loved with the thought it could be a waste of time as death may happen.

Here is my own story of the most traumatic experience I have had. I touched on it a little in the earlier chapter. A couple of years ago I wrote a post on Facebook, because I felt the need to share my situation in order to help someone who might be going through the same challenges.

My marriage was coming to an end and there was nothing I could do to get my wife and me back on the same page. I think when we go through a tragedy or separation from anything, whether it be from our kids, whether it be from relationships or our parents, we find ourselves at a crossroad not knowing which way to go. ?

And sometimes, we are unconscious of the decision we make when we're faced with this crossroads.

But at my crossroad, I was conscious and aware of where I wanted to go.

I realized we always got two paths, either we will go down the path of destruction, or we go down the path of enlightenment. And at that moment, in my lowest moment, my desire to go down the path of enlightenment spoke louder to me. I knew that I would come out a better man. Instead of taking the path of destruction that might have led to me possibly doing drugs or committing suicide I decided to become better version of myself and being a better version of myself meant a healthy mind and body. So, I escaped to the gym, and that's where I spent a lot of my time. I became obsessed with myself, constantly Working on myself, in order to make sure that I didn't mentally and emotionally fall apart.

I know that there's somebody out there right now, and you're at a crossroads wondering which way to go? Do you pick up a gun? Do you pick up a drug. You're at that crossroad, and you can self-destruct. or you can choose to better yourself?

You can focus more, you can find discipline, you can find wisdom, and you can find the good within a negative. Choose the road of enlightenment because you will become someone better. Someone on a whole different level, someone with some knowledge and some wisdom you can share and maybe inspire someone else. So focus and concentrate on yourself, and don't allow what you're going through to affect you negatively.

I tell you from the bottom of my heart, you matter! No matter what you think other people may think about you, no matter what you are going through, you matter to somebody somewhere, but ultimately you have to matter to yourself because then and only then can you reach the heights you're going to reach, and then and only then can you pull yourself up.

Once again, we all go through struggles in life. I know it can be hard. But It's all about how you approach it. How do you handle it? I know that crossroads is staring you dead in the face, and you can't see a way out but open your eyes to the truth you are much stronger than you think, open your heart to yourself.

Choose enlightenment because it's the best choice you can make.

Some traumas leave people physically handicapped besides the mental torture they will face. There are generally some traumas that are bigger than others, and this does not make some other person's traumatic experience less of one.

At times, our actions and behaviors result from certain traumatic experiences we had, some of which we may not term traumatic because it wasn't so dramatic. And others we are unaware of. But these behaviors seem to hunt us down and stop us from achieving or attaining success.

Answer these questions to discover the negative events from your past that may be influencing you today

1. What are your worst memories from childhood? This requires that you sit down and think. Try to remember incidents that happened to you or around you as a child. When you remember the incident well, you can then find out how those experiences affected you. Try to find out if you can link those incidents to any behavioral pattern you have. Also, try to find out if it changed your perspective on life and your thinking pattern in general. For example, someone who was sexually abused as a child will act in a certain way which may not be predicted as sexually abused victims handle the trauma in different ways. But generally, sexually abused victims approach life differently than those who weren't abused. Also, someone deprived of

love might find it difficult to accept love as they may feel undeserving. Try to find out if the experience made you make certain decisions then or later in life.

2.   What would you tell yourself if you could go back in time? With all the knowledge and experience you have, if you went back in time, what would you do differently? Would you change the course of things to avoid having that experience? If it has happened already, what advice or pep talk will you give yourself?

3.   Does it still impact you? Most traumatic experiences have a lifelong impact on their victims, ranging from disfigured bodies to a deterioration of mental health, nightmares, and many other things. So try to find out and answer if the experience still hunts you and still impacts your life.

4.   Are there other events that happened to you after childhood? Try to answer these questions too for those events that happened after childhood.

Traumatic events do not necessarily have to happen to an individual, but the person could be in the circumference of where it happened and get affected too.

People handle trauma differently. For some, they can shake it off and carry on with their lives. In cases like this, they may have no long-lasting effect on the incidence. For some others, they react to trauma differently. These events have a more profound effect on them. Our brains are so intent on protecting us that our responses to trauma can be extreme.

Some initial responses to trauma may include; confusion, anxiety, numbness, agitation, dissociation, sadness, etc. Some of these responses are mild and leave the victim fit to be part of society. Some severe responses may include; intense intrusive recollection even after being returned to safety, severe dissociation symptoms, and continuous distress without periods of relative calm or rest.

So delayed response could include; fatigue, sleep disorders, nightmares, fear of it reoccurring, etc.

These responses vary from individual to individual, and it depends on the severity of the event. Some events are more traumatic than others.

Depending on the severity of the event, here are things you might do to get yourself together once again

- Give yourself time. It may take time before you accept what happened. Give yourself that time. Do not pressure yourself or let anyone pressure you into accepting it when the time isn't right.

- Find out what happened. Especially when you are not directly involved. There are usually two sides to a story. Know exactly what happened.

- Be in with other survivors. In cases of natural disasters and accidents, get involved with others who survived.

- Ask for support. There is nothing wrong with asking for help. If you need help and support, do well to ask for it.

- Take some time for yourself. In case of the loss of a loved one, you might need some time alone with just yourself.

- Talk it over with someone. Find someone you can trust and talk it over with the person. This is therapeutic as talking with someone lifts some burden off your shoulder.

- Get into a routine. Take meals regularly, even if you do not feel like eating. Take walks and take your mind off the incident.

- Do normal things with others. You do not necessarily have to talk about what happened, but just being around others can help.

- Take care. It's been observed that those who have experienced trauma get into lots of accidents. Do take care to make sure you are not involved in an accident, especially at home.

For very severe cases, you must seek professional help, which might last a lifetime to enable you to live above it.

Traumas can create very limiting beliefs in us that will leave us almost useless on earth when not properly handled. These beliefs stop us from attaining the success we desire.

CHAPTER 10
ACTIVATION

TAKING ACTION

Did you actively participate in the last chapter's exercises? Then let's go!

Trance-formation starts from the mind. But trance-formation won't be useful or complete if the things learned are not applied in reality. You can never be transformed by imagining or tracing it in your head alone. There has to be a move. There has to be an action made. There has to be something that you do every day that would help you to be transformed, and that's the goal of this chapter to help you be truly trance-formed by taking action. But…

How does one know when they are trance-formed?

You would know if you were truly trance-formed when your life starts to reflect what your inner teacher told you to do. If your life hasn't manifested those inner attributes from your inner teacher, then you haven't started yet. But if the opposite, if you have written down everything said by your inner teacher, then you are good to go.

Steps to take action
Here are useful steps that you can apply when taking action

1. Start your day with an essential thing Now that you already have a visual representation of your new self-image in your mind and that of the one written down. Start each of your days by looking at the new self-paper. Remind yourself daily of

what you would like to become. Also, remind yourself about how you plan to get to your desired destination.

2. Take responsibility for your actions This is where you have to own full responsibility for any action you might take daily. Here you are fully in control of everything. Whatever you do or don't do would have setback consequences. Your responsibility for your actions is to ensure that everything you wrote down about your new self and your positive attributes should be constantly practiced else, they would die off, and you would lose out on all your efforts.

3. Take the first leap If you are still thinking of the perfect timing to practice what you have for your new self, you aren't waiting. Instead, you are wasting your time. Do you know why? It's because you would never find the perfect timing for such an activity. Even when you think you are free, you won't still find the time to do so. The wisdom there is to start small and take the first step. Start today! At your workplace, at home, at the club, start small. If your new self-image were to lose fat from your body, you can start applying your positive attributes now, do your exercise, take those gym lessons and start doing something right away before it is too late. Sometimes, you would feel emotionally down, you won't even feel like trying out something new, or you won't even feel motivated. But if you are determined, then the sky is never your limit.

4. Keep reminders I would write down the essential things I would like to focus on in my life. I would write them down and paste them on the walls and any other strategic location that can easily remind me. I even set alarms and online reminders that help remind me of important things I need to achieve in a day so that when the time comes, I would leave whatever I am doing and focus on practicing my new self-image. You can start by taking a paper and writing down the top three things in your life right now. You can write the most

important habit you would like to build in the next 30 days. You can even have a motto or quote to help you remain focused.

5. Be accountable to someone Yes, this might sound strange, but an accountability partner helps measure your progress level. Don't get me wrong; you can still measure your progress by comparing your old self with your new self. But an accountability partner would help make the workload much easier for you. Let the person be a friend close to you. Focus your energy on your new self

BONUS CHAPTER THROUGH THE FIRE, HANDLING RELAPSE

This chapter will be the shortest chapter as it will focus on handling specific situations.

In life, sometimes it seems like we are going back to those things which we fought so hard to avoid. For instance, someone who was into drugs and has started his journey into recovery can fall into a relapse where he goes back to taking drugs maybe just once. In times like this, he might feel that all hope is lost, and he cannot be helped because he feels he has gone back to his old ways.

There is a reason life is called a journey. It is full of ups and downs. Sometimes, you will have everything figured out, and sometimes, it seems like the whole world could end. Relapses are not just for those involved in drugs or alcohol, it cuts across all boards. You probably have experienced struggling with a habit and have gotten help along the way, and then boom, you go back and do that very same thing you are trying to save yourself from. Beating yourself up could only lead you back to that habit as you seek solace.

Below are ways you can handle a relapse

1.   Give yourself a pep talk This might sound cliché, but it always helps. Giving yourself a pep talk brings you to self-consciousness and awareness that anyone can fail at something and that failure isn't fatal. It can also breed confidence in you and help you overcome whatever you pass through. Handling relapses can help prevent or at least minimize the reoccurrence of what happened.

2. Talk to someone you trust Man was never designed to thrive in isolation, so we gravitate towards certain types of people. There should be someone you trust enough to talk to about what happened. It could be your therapist, family members, friends, or anyone who has gained your trust through what they have done for you and what they have done for others.

3. Have a support group A support group always helps if they are not always on the sad side of the coin. This is because if they are always on the sad side, they will be judgmental and could never provide real help. A support group helps you know that you are not alone in the struggle and can help each other together.

4. Quit worrying It is normal that during that point where you seem to have gone back to the bad habits, you will worry a lot. But then, worry has never solved an issue and never will. You will only sink deeper into whatever you are running from.

5. Hit the gym The gym is a good place to vent and release bad energy. By hitting the gym, you can clear your mind and produce better strategies to follow to help you out.

6. Have a little me time Learn to take a break and have time for yourself alone. This will help.

7. Take a trip A change of environment is a good way to get back on the right track. So pack your bags and take a trip to a new city or a new and different environment.

CONCLUSION

Knowing yourself is a challenging task. But knowing yourself is a fundamental key to success. Without self-knowledge, luck has a great influence over the results of our lives.

We comprise our values, experiences, habits, and preferences. The mistakes we make limit us. We are so busy worrying about the opinion of others that we do not know who we are anymore.

Our true self is the part that never changes. We often cover up our true selves with false beliefs and fears. We superimpose the desires of society on ourselves, so finding our true selves requires that take a hard look in the mirror and go back to the beginning.

Thank you so much for sharing your time with me on this journey to finding the man in you. Writing this book has been a journey of self-realization, and I hope you have enjoyed this book as much as I enjoyed writing it. I have always wanted to speak to a lot of people about the things I have experienced on my path to being the man I am today. This process has been very therapeutic for me.

To end this beautiful journey with you, I would like to share a little bit more of my story. I am the youngest of two children, with my elder sister as the first child. I was born and raised in Flint, Michigan. I love my city! Flint made my childhood worthwhile,It was beautiful, and I thank my mom and stepdad for all their sacrifices and hard work in raising me to be the man I am today. My stepfather was a pillar of strength in my life. He was everything a young boy would love to be in his older age. He was, in a way, a light unto my path, as he paved the way, leading me into being a good human being for myself and my family. He helped me develop into a man. He was a macho man, well, at least, he called himself that, hahaha. He served this country in the United States armed forces as a veteran of the Vietnam War. Regardless of how strict he could be, he was gentle and very protective of me. I learned a great deal of humility from him. He has since passed away, but he left me with a lot of jewels to always live by. There are so many, but here are some I can remember and share with you

"He who shits fast don't shit long." I can remember him saying this just like it was yesterday. He told me this to keep me out of the streets selling drugs. Drug money is fast money, and it means it comes fast and leaves even faster. You'll either end up dead or in jail.

Another one he would say was, *"A man is only as good as his word."* He would say this for the times I would mess up and ask me to give him my word that I would never let it happen again. It always worked like a charm. I always admired how he was so manly and respected; I wanted to be like that too, so I would always give him my word and stand by it. Every time was a trial, harder but more fulfilling than the next. Also, he would say if you give a man your word that you would do something, you must stand by your word and do it.

My relationship with my father is one of the typical circumstances. Although my mother and father were not together, my love for him knows no bounds. I have always had a deep and infinite love for my father, even though there are times when I wish he'd been more present. I now know this wasn't always possible, so I am always grateful for the times we spent together. They were very valuable to me. He is a unique man, and no matter what happens, he always stayed true to himself. I admired him just for being him. I love my dad for being himself!! My father gave me my identity. When I look into his eyes, I see me. It is just like I am looking in a mirror. But it runs deeper than looks.

Along with his beautiful soul, he has a great positive personality. He is a joy to be around, as he is loved by all and as he would tell you, feared by many. As funny as this sounds, this is true. His charisma is always shining, as much as his joyful zest for life. He was a hard worker then and is even harder working now, and although he had his own family, I always saw the love, loyalty, and devotion he had for them. That is one of the true definitions of a real man.

My father had no catchy phrases to give, but his actions and character spoke loud and clear. My dad is a hardworking man. He's in his sixties now and still going strong. He showed and taught me that hard work pays off, and if you do your best with everything, that's all that matters, and everything will be just fine. Every time we speak, it's almost like identical twins separated at birth. They finally see each other for the first time. It is amazing! We laugh alike, we walk alike, and sometimes, we even talk alike. I love my dad to death!!!

I have always loved the idea and having my own family and wanted to be a dad for as long as I can remember. I had always wanted a boy because I felt that if I had a boy, I could relive a little bit of my childhood, and I could make up for the time I lost with my dad. I also felt I would break the generational curse plaguing the Black Father and Son relationship. God has given me my opportunity, and I will make great use of it. As I write this book, my son is nine years old, and no matter my circumstance, I will not let anything come between us. All these life experiences I have shared with you on these pages, although at times seem to be curses conjured up by some evil witch, turns out they be blessings in disguise. Go figure! So to sum it all up, this is who I am. **I AM A SON, A FATHER, but ULTIMATELY, I AM A MAN.** I stand firm in my truth and am here to help you stand firm in yours. And when they doubt you or when you even doubt yourself, take a hard look in the mirror. You know the look! The

one where you cock ya head back, tilt it to the side, grab ya balls
and ask ya self, Who's the Man?

Made in the USA
Middletown, DE
29 October 2023

41493949R00036